GW00537106

When Upton Had Trains

A Memoir of the Village of Upton
during the 1950s and 1960s
in
Short Essays and Verse

This edition published in 2008 by Natula Publications
Natula Ltd., Christchurch, Dorset BH23 1JD

ISBN 9781897887752

A CIP catalogue record of this book is available from the British Library.

Printed by Cpod, Trowbridge, Wiltshire.

Front Cover Illustration:
Goods train pictured about 250 yards from Poole Road railway gates on the Hamworthy Junction to Upton line with the Dorset Clay Products factory in the background c. 1963-64.
© Alan Burridge

Back Cover Illustration:
Steam train at Poole High Street level crossing c. 1963-64.
© Robert Burridge

All other photographs from the author's collection.

Contents

The Millennium Clock, Upton Crossroads

Introduction

Our lives move even faster these days, modern technology and global logistics have ensured our world runs at a much quicker rate. Yet half a century ago, things moved at a far steadier pace, and seemingly, no one suffered at those slower hands going around on the face of the very same clock, ticking our lives away as steadily as it still does.

The inspiration for getting these reminiscences together has been a local magazine to this, my home town of Upton, by the name of *The Lytchett Bay Post*, which is published by Jayne Blight. After reading the first issue and then making myself known to Jayne, she asked, as I had introduced myself as a writer, if I had anything to contribute? As ever, the mind goes blank on such an occasion, not, I hasten to add due to the fabled writers' block. No, I had a lot of work on, yet by the time the second edition was published my way had cleared a little, so I wrote a couple of humorous poems about our village of Upton.

After emailing them through to Jayne, she replied saying she liked them enough to publish, and did I have any features or articles? So I rewrote a couple of essays which had appeared as 'blogs', followed by a couple of originals. It was also quite fun to walk the length and breadth of the village taking photographs to illustrate the essays; something I have never done enough of, despite being advised to do so after a fairly recent heart operation.

Jayne printed *Upton Crossroads for Visitors* in the Winter issue; *The Village Idiot* in the Spring edition with *Upton In Bloom* and the essays as and when they would fit. Fired up by the enthusiastic nostalgia, after 20 or so poems, I began writing even more essays about reminiscences of Upton from the 1950s onwards, thinking they may also be of interest? They were. Then, always keen on books about Poole and the surrounding area, I found Natula Publications on an Amazon search, who had printed quite a number of books, mainly about the Christchurch locality; but would they consider something about Upton?

Fortunately, Natula were happy to spread their wings into the Upton area, so here we have those short essays and the twenty or so witty poems, which I hope, if you are new to the village, will enlighten you, and if you have lived here all of your life, remind you of our past.

People are born, they grow up, get married, move away or stay put, then pass on. Everything is changing constantly, so this is how Upton <u>was</u> back then - not necessarily <u>better</u>, but vastly <u>different</u>.

Alan Burridge 2008

The Author

Alan Burridge has written since he was able, but has done so regularly for the rock group, Motorhead, as their Fan Club organiser, since 1980. During that time he has published over 80 fanzines and written 3 books on the band, and is now working on a biography. Along with writing 7 (now out-of-print) fictional crime thrillers based in the Upton and Poole areas, he is also a Top 500 reviewer for the Amazon website, and has written well over a hundred gig reviews for the *Mr Kyps* live music venue in Parkstone, as well as verse and short essays for local community magazines.

Living in Upton for the majority of his life and happily married to Jane since 1973, they have 2 children and 7 grandchildren.

www.alanburridge.freeuk.com

Dedicated with Thanks to My Three Jane's

Jayne Blight for the inspiration;

Jane Burridge for the encouragement;

Jane Martin for the faith to publish.

Visit www.natula.co.uk for their catalogue of local interest books.

A Bit o' Witty Verse about Upton

Upton Crossroads for visitors

Upton Crossroads has been in my life, for fifty years or over,
And a café called The Mont Dor, used to stand upon the corner,
Where trucks and lorry driver's stopped, it was a greasy spoon,
And we'd sit outside listening, to rock 'n' roll jukebox tunes.

Where the Poole Road flats are, was the house of Doctor Chown,
Who diagnosed my appendicitis, when on his village rounds,
And my tummy ached so awful, it made me feel so glum,
But not as much as his finger, when he stick it up my…

But that's how they find out what is wrong, it's how it has to be,
So let's move on to Hicks grocery shop, by the clump of trees,
Adjacent to The Greenridge, a public house of some repute,
Where I had my first drink of beer, and then sicked it down me suit.

It was called The Upton Hotel then, but this you may not recall?
Cos Upton's changed quite a bit, and you must be on the ball,
Like the Blue Star Garage used to be, where the Millennium Clock
now stands,
And it'll tell you what time of day it is, if you have some on your
hands.

Upton is my metropolis, and the village where I was born,
And I have enjoyed it through my lifetime, in its numerous,
changing forms,
So if you see the signpost, drive off the bypass, come and say 'Hello',
We won't bite, I promise, but there again, you never know?

Yes, we had trains!

Born in 1951, Upton was rather different as a child than it is now, of course. Quaintly, I rather like to parallel it with the world Agatha Christie portrays in the *Miss Marple* television programmes, particularly with the late Joan Hickson playing the leading role. It was a world of comparative peace, as if everyone was breathing a huge sigh of relief after living through two World Wars in fairly rapid succession and hoped another would not follow just as closely as no one knew what was in store. It was also a world of immense honesty and trust, and quite a few years before homes had TV or music centres, so no one had anything worth stealing, anyway. And although that world was far from perfect, as Miss Marples' murder-solving and two World Wars had proven, people were far more agreeable and polite, and day-to-day living had a freshness and zest because of it.

And we dressed much as they did in the Miss Marple films, too, and few but the village practitioner, Doctor Chown, owned a car, and the word *cancer* would be quietly mouthed on a hushed breath rather than actually spoken, if, indeed, anyone had need to say it. This was in the days before the link between smoking and cancer had been exposed. People smoked; it was part of every-day-life and it wasn't considered a 'crime' or life-threatening then. The main reason not to smoke or cut down would be a financial one; it was an expense families could ill-afford. It would, perhaps, be just the one cigarette after the evening meal; so a packet of 20 would last 20 days; and even then, often it would be forgotten or not bothered with, so they may have lasted for a month or more.

Yes, Upton was this quiet and tiny village slightly the

worse-for-wear after those two World Wars, where everyone knew everyone else and if you didn't attend church on Sunday you were rather frowned upon, as it was regarded as *the* social place to go. And no one had much else to do, anyway, and it was something of a nice change for everyone to put on their best clothes, which were mostly hand made at home on a sewing machine by the mothers and grandmothers, to go and sing and say a few prayers and use the escapism of the Church to forget our world outside and hope for a better future.

Poole Road, Upton c.1900

During those war years, with the Admiralty munitions factory at Holton Heath, most of the women of Upton and Lytchett Minster walked or cycled there to work during the week. It was what they did and were expected to do so for the 'War Effort'. They would have their hair tied up in a scarf, and were not permitted to wear hair pins, earrings or brooches of

2

any kind for fear if one fell to the floor and created a spark, it would have blown them, and the factory, to smithereens.

The Admiralty Munitions Factory, Holton Heath

Of course, the factory was also a target for enemy aircraft, and a 'dummy' model of it was built from wood and cardboard and situated on the Isle of Arne to detract the foe from the real thing, and thankfully, it did. But there had been dog-fights with the enemy in the Upton skies already. The area now known as Greenacre Close, off Yarrells Lane, was a small pine forest. Amidst its dark and spooky interior there were two immense blossoms of bright light where the Stuka aircraft had dropped their bombs willy-nilly to aid their aerial manoeuvrability and blown up quite a large number of the trees and had only just missed hitting the crossroads in doing so!

The enemy planes dumped those bombs anywhere just to get rid of them, especially if their strike had been rumbled by Britain's defences. Ideally, they should have hit the ammunition factory, of course, but Spitfire and Hurricane aircraft would be scrambled from Tarrant Rushton, an airfield near Badbury Rings, to try to stop them, which they succeeded in doing.

Also, on the heath to the right of Blandford Road North, was the Upton Gun Site, where 'Pom-Pom' anti-aircraft guns were located as a further defence for the Holton Heath factory. When the air-raid siren sounded with its eerie banshee wail, locals in the Home Guard would run, often from their beds as the attacks usually took place at night, to man the guns and assist the fighter aircraft in blowing the enemy planes from the Upton skies.

The air-raid siren was located in the small woodland copse between what is now the *Custom Kitchens* shop next door to *Palmer Snell Estate Agents,* and *The Greenridge* public house; and was housed at the top of a scaffolding-like structure. From time-to-time, even in those early post-war years, the siren would be tested to ensure it still worked, as no one knew if and when it would ever be needed again. It was eventually taken down and removed.

Parallel to the main Blandford Road, from Hamworthy Junction, (which is now part of the Country Walk), was the railway line going to Broadstone and beyond. Adjacent to what is now the 'Crossways' lane and *Layers* Hairdressers shop, were the railway gates and a small signal box, and a fair few trains used the line on a daily basis.

Hence, some of the train times would conflict with local people going to or returning from work, and the gates would be the focus of a curse from many a man made late by their closure. And can you just imagine the look on the faces of the Upton children of today if they could stand and watch a hulking great steam train going across that piece of tarmac? It would be *magic!*

Remnant of the Railway Line, Upton Woods

The Upton railway line

From the junction down at Hamworthy, to Broadstone and beyond,
The trains that came through Upton, of which we were quite fond,
With billowing smoke, and thunderous noise, rattling on the lines,
The day they went and took it away, it was an awful crime.

At twenty-to-eight, it woke us up, better than any clock,
Or any other waking device, including a farmyard cock,
Rattling and a rolling, through Upton in the mist,
And now there's barely evidence, that they ever did exist.

It filled us with awe and wonder, as it would the kids of today,
They wouldn't need a computer, to while their time away,
The smell of steam was wonderful, a pleasure to everyone's nose,
But even so, there'd be some moans, if the railway gates were closed.

To see this fiery monster, chuffing across the Poole Road,
In the summer or the winter, in the rain or in the snow,
It didn't seem to matter, those days were never drab,
Waving at the smiling engine driver, up there in the cab.

But now those days are gone, and some villagers can't recall,
Those mighty, steaming engines, so wide and long and tall,
And how they thundered through so loud, drowning out your talk,
But the evidence is still there to see, along the Country Walk.

But don't you go a lingering, if you're down there walking the dog,
Especially if it's autumn, and you get caught in the morning fog,
And you might think I'm kidding, when I tell you these Upton tales,
But listen hard and you'll hear those ghosts, rattling along the rails.

Hungry and cold

With those of us fortunate enough to have had fathers returning from the Second World War, the Force's training and discipline instilled within them ensured times were strict; how could they not be? Times were also hungry. Most families in Upton had a large back garden, growing as much of the food to be put onto the table as possible, as well as rearing chickens for their precious eggs, so the plot would be regarded as a smallholding.

During the earlier war years, even the lawns had been dug up to accommodate crops like potatoes, greens and fruit bushes. The UK is an island, and during the Second World War especially, with U-Boats prowling the Atlantic, we had to be self-sufficient, as very little, if anything, from abroad would get through on a ship as they would be torpedoed and sunk.

So we grew up being gardeners, digging, planting and fertilising the soil with the manure from the chickens and kitchen waste. The Summers were great, and usually hot, even though we had a few bad ones from time to time, as we still do now. But the Winter's were freezing, and with the words 'central heating' not yet in our vocabulary, the evenings would be spent listening to the wireless (radio), playing cards or reading and writing, whilst sitting as close to the open coal fire as possible. Chilblains would inevitably be the result of this indulgence, and *Snow-Fire* chilblain cream would be in every home to combat this common ailment.

Getting up on a frosty Winters morning was truly a bitter experience and, as 'double glazing' had also not yet been invented, most of the windows would be iced-up both inside and out! Overnight, the fire would have extinguished itself, of course, so a portable stove, which burned paraffin, would be brought into the front room or lounge, placed in the hearth and lit. On weekdays, fresh from our bed and dressed in pyjamas and dressing gown, shivering we would change into our school clothes which felt as if even they had spent the night hanging on the washing line in the garden.

That done, breakfast might be cereal, toast and dripping or both. Dripping, for the sake of younger readers, was the fat from the Sunday meat roast, solidified and spread on toast or even plain bread. Like the Eskimo, the fat helped keep us warm. My abiding memory of Winters in Upton, from the age of 4 to perhaps 11, was the bitter cold, yet it was no fault of my parents. Every home suffered the same; families just had an open fire in the one room and that was it.

The milk would be delivered by the local dairy's milkman, *Plumleys* or *Arnolds*, as there was no other way of getting it. With the cold so intense, by the time we got up to fetch the milk from the doorstep, the cream would have solidified pushing the tin-foil lid off, enabling the blue tits and other small birds to peck at the cream to get *their* little bit of fat to keep *them* warm and alive.

Generally, the refrigerator had yet to be installed in the majority of people's kitchens and most families had what was called a 'safe' instead. A 'safe' was a wooden cupboard on legs, with finely-meshed wire set into the door and both sides. It would be sited facing towards the Northerly direction, and it was regarded as 'safe' inasmuch as the milk, cheese and meat inside it could be kept 'safe' from flies or hungry cats or dogs, whilst being kept fresh at the same time. However, there was a dramatic increase in the sale of refrigerators during the long hot Summer of 1959.

Most Winter mornings, as we ate breakfast, I would have my plate on the window sill, and sat there looking at the patterns and shapes in the ice on the window panes. Those designs are still fascinating to this day when they are on the car with those incredible shapes and designs like weird science fiction flowers, strange ferns and trees.

Sums, or maths, would never be my great strongpoint, but I couldn't wait to read and write. Writing came along hand-in-hand with the rare times we watched TV. Both sets of grandparents had one, bought during the 1953 'TV Boom' in order to watch The Queen's Coronation, but we didn't have one for quite a while.

When we visited either grandparents we would take along a notebook and pencil, and write down the names of the advertisers during the commercial breaks. This may sound boring to most, and *Typhoo* tea and *Omo* washing powder and so on were hardly a great deal to write about, but doing so made writing something enjoyable to do, which would end up being a life-long passion, so it probably started at that point from those humble seeds.

Every day, my brother Robert would read the 'Sooty' cartoon from the *Daily Mirror*, and I would pester him until he taught me, so I could read fairly well when I started school, which was at Upton Infants. Miss Bags was the Headmistress and the teachers were Mrs Johnson and Miss Peach.

At the time, my Granddad, Walter Burridge, was caretaker at the school, which meant he did all the odd jobs including attending to the boiler house. Life was changing; school actually had this new-fangled thing called 'central heating' so it was worth going just to be warm all day.

Again, it was probably a throwback from the war, but

every time an airplane was heard in the distance, the whole school would run outside onto the playing field to look at it. Whether our teachers were checking if it was an enemy or a friendly aircraft, none of us even considered, but I suppose this may have been the case? Had it been an enemy plane perhaps there was an air raid shelter nearby which they would have rushed us into?

My most vivid memories from Upton Infants' School are Mrs Johnson reading aloud from a book titled *The Magic Toffee*, her slapping my backside because I was always looking out of the classroom window and knocking my front teeth out in a playground accident.

Most young people have probably heard and laughed about the older generation telling of how they would get an orange and a knob of coal for their Christmas present. Well, it wasn't quite that bad for our generation, but I could not do without a notebook and a pencil for mine, bearing in mind that fountain pens then were extremely primitive and messy things and the 'Biro' was still not yet in general circulation.

So I would read from that early start my brother gave me, and write all sorts of strange, juvenile stories in the notebook just because I enjoyed the act of writing, whilst always being puzzled at how they managed to get the text straight on both sides of the page in the books I read.

Although we didn't realise it, we were so fortunate having the railway line from Hamworthy Junction through to Broadstone and beyond at the top of the garden. What an absolute delight for children! To be honest, we didn't even know at the time where anything *beyond Broadstone* might have been. We were aware this place named Broadstone existed, but with travel the way it was at the time, we had never actually been there, or indeed, ever had a reason to consider going.

Train in Broadstone Station, 1950s

Our Mother, Audrey, wrote to *Fry's* chocolate factory in Bristol one year and as a family during the school Summer Holiday we went there by train for a guided tour and plenty of samples. My brother reminded me that on the return journey the train brought us home along the line from Broadstone to Hamworthy Junction and enabled us to actually ride on the railway line behind where we lived.

The Upton Women's Institute

Back then there was no 'pre-school', so you spent your time with
Mum,
So wherever she went, so did you, and some of it wasn't much fun,
And even though I was less than five years old, deep within me was
a guy,
Who used to dread the weekly visit, to the Upton W.I.

It was a great big Nissan hut, on the left, in Ropers Lane,
And once you'd been there once, you didn't really want to go again,
And we'd sit there being seen not heard, as kids had to at the time,
And if you squeaked or made a sound, it was virtually a crime.

They'd sit there talking about knitting, recipes and strawberry jam,
And how to hang and cook a pheasant, or roast a leg of lamb,
Then sing while Mrs Oxborough played, the jingly old piano,
A hymn or some religious thing, to keep them on the straight and
narrow.

And then they'd get out this tea pot, as big as an elephant's head,
And make this tea-like-creosote, that you could paint on your garden
shed,
But after sitting there in silence, meditation, and being alone,
It was an oasis in a desert of chatter, and it meant we were going
home.

But it gave Mum and Gran a boost, a weekly social event,
And every woman with no exceptions, made sure that she went,
But I was glad in some ways, cos you felt an outcast and a fool,
When finally the day arrived, when I could go to school.

Cos it meant no more W.I., a place males don't belong,
The only highlight was that cup of tea, so sweet and hot and strong,

And when I came home after that, from school, and gave Mum a
kiss,
I smiled if it was Wednesday, because I knew exactly what I'd
missed.

**The Lytchett Crossing & Village, Upton
at the turn of the 20th Century**

Chicken feed

So, Broadstone and beyond was something of a mystery, much like Corfe Mullen, Wimborne and most of the other 'local' villages. Imagine not having a car; *Tesco* at Fleetsbridge or *Asda* in town would be quite some haul by public transport, especially as the bus service wasn't as good then as it is today, then perhaps you can understand why such easy-to-get-to local places as they are now, seemed so far away.

The Railway Station at Hamworthy Junction

We kept chickens and they would be fed on corn or, other than having any scraps the dog or cat wouldn't eat, potato peelings would be steamed in the pressure cooker and mixed and mashed in an old bowl with a powdered feed called 'meal' which the chickens would then eagerly devour. But the corn and the 'meal' had to come from somewhere and that would be *Hoopers* the coal merchants, whose yard was in Galloway Road, now behind the fire station.

To get there and bring a fresh half-hundredweight (25kg) sack of each home as chicken feed, we had a cart made from a stout wooden crate with an old set of pram wheels and a pair of handles attached. Robert, Mum and I would set off down the Blandford Road to fetch them. Turlin Moor did not exist at this time, and to get to Hamworthy Junction there was a dirt, gravel track wide enough to take a car, which led past *Strong & Co of Romsey* imaginatively named *Station Hotel*. A pedestrian footpath had been worn away as an offshoot from this, taking the walker, and us with our barrow, through the station underpass into Galloway Road.

Once in *Hooper's* yard, Mrs. Hooper would emerge from the house to meet us, have a quick yarn with Mum and between us we would load these two bags of feed into the cart, then walk them back home. Chicken were rather good at recycling, and would eat any spare greens which happened to be cut from a home-grown cabbage, or the weeds from the garden; virtually anything in fact, and the resulting nutrients would end up in those beautiful, fresh-from-the-nest-box eggs.

On even a half-decent day, we would think nothing of walking to Hamworthy to see Gran's sister, Doris, or even all the way into Poole to do some shopping.

Poole Bus Station consisted of a rough, flat piece of concrete, (which is now Kingland Crescent, situated between the railway gates and the *H. Samuel's* entrance to the Dolphin Centre) with half-a-dozen bus stops, and much like today, we would queue at the appropriate one.

The land the Dolphin Centre is now built on was a flat piece of grass called 'Lady's Walking Field', where Summer would usually bring a circus or a fair. One of my most awful memories of visiting such an event was being bought a candyfloss, which (just my luck) had a wasp in it, and it stung my tongue - not very nice at all! There were tears before bedtime that day without a doubt!

Poole High Street c.1950s

Wash day was always on Monday, and Gran had a copper in which to boil the water, a wash-board to scrub the clothes on, a large pair of tongs to stop her hands and fingers getting scalded when she turned the clothes in the copper and a little blue bag of whatever-it-was which reputedly made the clothes whiter! Oh, and a huge, floor-standing cast-iron mangle with wooden rollers and a massive handle to wring the water from the clothes to enable them to dry quicker.

Starting early, 'the washing' would take the best part of the morning to do, and with luck and weather permitting, Gran would have it hanging on the line by midday. Believe you me, the women in those days had quite some muscles on them, moving saturated washing around and lifting it up to put it through a mangle most certainly built up their strength.

Our middle, or 'junior school' as we knew it, was situated adjacent to Lytchett Minster Church, as indeed the buildings still are. Mr Rogers was headmaster and Mrs Leyman was the teacher for the 1st and 2nd years, Miss Viney the 4th. However, the 3rd year would be the one every male child from the village learned to dread, because it would be with Mr Jenkins, whose fearful reputation preceded him.

On the last day before going back to school after the Summer Holiday, it was always a miserable task having to 'dubbin' the football boots, as it was the final realisation that yes, those Summer Holidays really had ended. And for me it was in September 1960 that I had to go back to school with 'Jenko', as he was known by all the kids, as my form master. This I did with feelings bordering upon the will to commit suicide to avoid it and him borne most strongly in mind. Of course, that was not and never has been an option in my life, so the term began much the same as it always had, with every boy going into Jenko's year quaking in their boots.

The disused railway line, Upton

17

Train ride to the end of the world

It should be appreciated, that some fifty years ago,
Our world was somewhat different, and things moved along quite
slow,
So when our Granddad said he would take us, to Southampton for
the day,
It was like going to India, or America, cos it seemed a thousand
miles away.

Just going to Bournemouth, shopping, was an expedition for all
concerned,
And the people in the shops and streets moved much faster, so we
learned,
So Southampton with its lights and shops and fluttering flags
unfurled,
Was so scary yet exciting, like a train ride to the end of the world.

And so we'd go, but didn't know, if ever we'd be coming back home,
We'd grab hold tight to Granddad's hand, it wasn't wise to roam,
And board the train at Poole Station, whistles blew and flags were
waved,
We were excited young adventurers, so honest, trusty and brave.

Lunch at some High Street restaurant was like a banquet fit for a
King,
And we would eat all put before us, we didn't waste a single thing,
Then we'd thank our great big Granddad, for such a wonderful day
out,
We had more shops to look at, time went too fast without a doubt.

He'd buy us a bag of roasted peanuts, to eat going home on the train,
And we would be quite certain, next year he'd be taking us again,
And other than Christmas Day, this was the highlight of our year,

Making Granddad very special, whom in our hearts was very dear.

We would get back home exhausted, ready for a bath and then to
bed,
Mum and Dad would always ask us, if there was somewhere else
instead,
Of Southampton, that we'd like to go, with Granddad, next year on
the train?
But no, we enjoyed that day so much we'd like to go back there
again.

The scourge of Leonard Jenkins

Today, Mr Leonard 'Jenko' Jenkins, 3rd year teacher at Lytchett Minster Junior School, would not get away with the way he treated us, and by and large, perhaps, more is the pity? On the one hand he was a fantastic teacher; we had weekly trips to the old, open-air and unheated Poole Baths where he taught many of us to swim; more by fear than skill, admittedly, but he did it, nevertheless.

A big fan of *Bell Boy* bubble gum, available from *Hicks* the village grocery shop at 4 for 1 penny, or a farthing each, I had blown a bubble on the way to school and it had burst and stuck to my chin. An attempt at hiding it through Assembly failed as the eagle-eyed Jenko spotted something was wrong, wheedled me out of the throng and took me to one side during one of the hymns. At seeing the problem, he marched me to the galley-style cloakroom, which also had washbasins and connected the old part of the school to the new. There, he found an awful, vomit-smelling cloth, wetted it under the tap, dipped it in some *Vim* and scrubbed the gum from my chin, which after his all-too vigorous efforts went as red as a cherry for the remainder of the day.

Jenko also ensured we knew our multiplication tables, and again, used the tactic of unbridled fear to do this. As a form, we would chant them en-mass, then he would prowl the classroom, 12" ruler in hand, to ask individuals "Nine eights?" or whatever. The ruler would be gently slid through the pupil's hair from front to back, positioned so that you were looking Jenko right in the eye and then he would begin tapping the ruler on your skull. And the longer you took answering, the harder the tapping became and eventually

20

began to hurt so every pupil *made sure* they knew their times tables *and* everything else taught to avoid this nasty punishment by Mr Leonard Jenkins.

Michael Howard sat in the front row of the classroom. Jenko would walk in after Assembly, call the Register and then order Howard to join him at the front of the classroom. With our PE bags holding shorts, T-shirt and plimsolls hanging on the back of our chairs, he would say, "Ellis! Plimsoll!" Duncan Ellis would do as he had been ordered, and remove one plimsoll from his PE bag and hand it to our teacher.

Lytchett Minster Junior School

Taking a piece of blackboard chalk, Jenko would mark 3 crosses on the sole of the gym shoe. Howard knew by now to bend over, as he suffered this *every single day,* and we would sit there cringing on his behalf. Unfortunately for Michael

21

Howard, he had something of a lazy attitude, slouched when he walked and had a generally idle disposition, and simply because he could, Jenkins would 'slipper' Howard every morning before doing anything else. As he slippered him, we would receive a vocal commentary along the lines of: "Howard!" whack, "In Wales," whack, "the pit-ponies," whack, "won't work," whack, "unless we beat them," whack, "and you're just like them, Howard," whack, "so I have to," whack, "beat you every day," whack, "to get you moving!" whack. "Now sit down, Howard!"

Jenkins' face had turned blood red; eyes would be bulging and his ginger/brown curly hair a mess from his exertions. That man put every ounce of strength into every whack he gave a male pupil and I believe he thoroughly enjoyed doing it. He only had the one daughter, Sally Anne, and would never have slippered her, so he took his wrath out on the boys in his form every year.

But like Howard, I also found out on several occasions that you didn't just get 3 whacks. Oh no; Jenko beat your backside with this gym-shoe until he matched up the 3 chalk crosses, so you could have 8 or maybe 10 whacks, or until he felt satisfied you had suffered the required punishment. Believe me, after having a stumpy, thick-set Welshman give you 8 or more of those you could barely stand, walk, or sit down. And if you cried, well, you just didn't or else the other members of the class, mainly the girls, whom he never slippered, would call you "cry baby bunting" or whatever, so it wasn't worth it. However, if tears were not seen you were regarded as something of a hero, and mine never were, but holding back has played havoc with my emotions ever since. So thank you Mr Jenkins for messing up my life!

Mr Jenkins was every boy's worst nightmare at junior school, but he made sure you learned *everything* simply by being scared of the penance suffered if you didn't pay attention and learn. Today, he would probably be arrested for what he did with Ellis' plimsoll, but *I know* the streets of not only Upton, but the whole of the UK would be far safer and with less trouble on them if the Mr Jenkins of our old world could return. What he did may not have been right, but it made the younger generation respect their elders. This is one major aspect our society lacks today, unfortunately. *Long Live Mr Jenkins!*

Any punishment at school had to be kept secret from your parents because if they found out a teacher had reprimanded you, there would be another good telling-off when you got home for playing up at school and bringing the family name into disrepute.

Michael Kimber's conkers

At Junior School next to Lytchett Church, playtime was quite glum,
But better than being in the classroom, doing those endless sums,
Then Miss Viney would blow her whistle, and we'd all stand in line,
And file back to those classrooms, and do our best to shine.

None of us were the brightest sparks, just average in our IQs,
And school went on for weeks like this, with far more don'ts than
do's,
But when Autumn term came along, all the boys went bonkers,
When Michael Kimber struggled in with a monstrous bag of conkers.

He lived up the road, on a great big farm, a horse chestnut on the
plot,
And when those conkers started to fall, at lunchtime, off he'd trot,
To walk back in with that great big bag, swinging at his side,
And the kids would bubble around him, like a swirling, expectant
tide.

He'd stand there by the climbing frame, kids' eyes shining with
delight,
And he'd open that bag and chuck 'em, and there'd often be a fight,
In that screaming and snatching frenzy, for conkers, by the boys,
When they all went quite barmy, and made such an awful noise.

So while those conker's were in season, Michael Kimber was the
man,
And if he could have driven one, he would have brought them in a
van,
And every year he did it, throwing conkers by the score,
But we've grown up, and so has he, and don't need them any more.

Never bored

The words are so familiar and are so tedious I could scream.

"I'm bored!"

That's what the kids of today continually annoy us with, and also keep us in the red at the bank and up to the limit on our credit cards. Just like everyone else, I used to cringe and my skin would creep when one of my grandparents referred to their youth and teenage years as 'the good old days'. Dare I say it, but I used to think they were *boring* when they reminisced like that, yet now I find myself doing much the same. But in our post-war world, where if you didn't have the money *in hard cash,* you couldn't buy what you wanted, it had to be better, didn't it?

In many ways, I feel sorry for the kids of today and as my 10-year-old son said, quite rightly, when I screamed at him, "Why do you want all this stuff?" he meekly answered, "Because they put it there for me to want!" Today, there are far too many things for the children of today to *want,* and either via that overdraft or 'spanking the plastic', they seem to get what they are after just to shut them up. Yet in my 'good old days' there was not such a bewildering array of toys available and so rather than 'getting bored', we would amuse ourselves - somehow.

Okay, we were not completely hard done-by and bereft of everything. We had comics like *Victor, Lion, Tiger and Eagle* and a *Hornby* train set; we had *Dinky Toys* and also the *Matchbox* cars and lorries and like my son, they were there for us to want, too, but without the facility of *credit,* we had to *save up* to buy what we were after.

In the meantime, we would spend the Summer holiday in the back garden, either our own or that of a neighbouring friend or relation. Sometimes we would weed part of the garden, cut the lawn, hoe-up the spuds, muck out the chickens, or just quite simply be the young idiots we were and jump off the shed roof onto the compost heap. Dad used to go berserk because we would get a small camp fire going and burn his precious pea sticks and runner bean rods for fuel. Yet despite that, we were *trusted* to be left all day long with that camp fire as both he and mum worked! (Dad at the Upton Brickworks and Mum at *Hicks'* grocery shop).

We had the railway line behind the properties and other than watching the trains going by or shunting, when everything was clear we would walk back towards Hamworthy Junction, hoping not to get caught (as it was Private Property and a *dangerous* place to be) and would run like the clappers if anyone spotted us. It was easy to tell when a train was due, as there was a wire running alongside the line to the signal, so when the signal went up to indicate a train was on its way, the rarely-oiled wire would squeak, which gave us some time to either get back home or hide.

Also in those Summer holidays, two men would gradually work their way along the side of the tracks, with a crooked stick and scythe, cutting down the grass. Inevitably, as it dried out over the next few weeks, a hot piece of coal would become blown out of the trains' funnel as it chuffed past and land in the dry, cut grass catching it alight. We would beat it out as best we could. But this was all part of the fun, and we enjoyed ourselves immensely doing such things.

Where Allens Road is now, and covered with bungalows and houses, then it was just a flat, barren plain of clay-riddled earth with the odd tuft of grass here and there stretching as far as the ECM building (recently demolished). The ECM building to the left of the first red-bricked railway arch housed ECM Ltd. which sold ex-army trucks, jeeps and personnel carriers. Who bought these vehicles, I don't know, but they were there parked in rows behind the chain-link fence like a post-war ex-Forces vehicle car sales lot.

Opposite, where the maisonettes have been built, there was a huge, caged area full of old tyres from army vehicles, stacked up so high against the embankment they almost reached the railway line above. It seemed as if there were thousands of them and there probably were.

Poole Power Station in the 1950s

Yes, we were being naughty boys walking down the railway line, and we used to put stones on the rails and laugh when they became crunched to powder as the train went over them but we were *never* bored!

If it did happen to start creeping into our lives during those six, heavenly weeks away from school, we would walk to Turlin Moor recreation ground to play a daft game we called 'Best Man Fall'. There would usually be me, my brother, cousin Richard and neighbourhood pal, John Westacott. One of us would lie at the base of the steep incline going up to the flat, grass-topped field whilst the other three would jog towards the edge. The boy at the bottom would pretend to 'shoot' the three boys as they appeared over the grassy horizon, they would then roll down the embankment and 'the shooter' would judge who fell best (like the only heroes we had at the time: The Lone Ranger and Roy Rogers). The boy chosen would then take over to 'shoot' the other three and so it went on. This we found to be tremendous fun, simple and daft as it was, but we were never bored, rarely fought with each other, were darned good friends, and still are to this day.

To be honest, I think just by way of the fact that we were not at school was enough, we found school *boring* or at least I did, and the Summer holiday, which wasn't, like all good things always came to an end far too quickly.

Turlin Moor recreation ground was created from the earth dug out for the footings for the Power Station and the roads, walls, hedges and hedgerows of the Blandford Road and beyond were white with dust from the stone the *Shillingstone Lime Company* lorries were taking for infill in its place.

If Mrs Dacombe knew

It was a big house like 'The Munsters' had, and just as dark and
                                                            creepy,
Situated in our village, which some regard as sleepy,
But the paper boy, he feared that path, the worst one on his round,
But Christmas it was worth it, cos she'd give him half a crown.

A mighty Monkey-Puzzle tree, stood in Mrs Dacombe's garden,
Amidst the overgrown shrubbery, which begged nobody's pardon,
Some kids thought she was a witch, who'd turn us into slugs and
                                                            snails,
That woman was surrounded by, so many odd village tales.

But through this monumental fear, the village was brought to shame,
When a man went in and murdered her, then ran off down the lane,
Police and detectives were everywhere, asking where we'd been and
                                                    where we were?
And then asking us all over again, just in case we weren't too sure.

But in the end they caught him, and off he went in a prison van,
He'd spent the money he'd stolen, such a nasty kind of man,
But Mrs Dacombe's life lives on, when they put her name to
                                                    Dacombe Drive,
So she's much more famous now she's dead, than she ever was alive!

Honor Blackman

The Upton Liberal Hall and adjoining grounds used to be on the present and rather aptly named 'Clayfields' housing development, in Poole Road. The Upton Liberal candidate usually wins the local elections and it has always been a two-horse race with a Conservative also in the running; it has never been worth Labour even bothering to stand. But putting politics to one side, the Upton Liberal Fête was always worth attending, one way or another, every Summer in the village.

In the very early 1960s, The Right Honourable Earl of Mayo was our Liberal candidate and somehow he or the Party managed to secure the services of film and TV star Honor Blackman, to open the fête. (A year or two later she starred as 'Pussy Galore' in *Goldfinger*.) This was quite some coup for the village to say the very least.

My brother and I have always been very keen photographers and after many years of black & white films, I had managed to save up my paper round and pocket money, bought the latest and state-of-the-art *Kodak Instamatic* camera and loaded it with my very first colour slide film. Mum and Dad may well have helped out buying the film for this rather special occasion, for after all when, before or since, has anyone as famous as Honor Blackman ever set foot in Upton, never mind opened the Summer Fête?

As small a population as the village had then, everyone but *everyone* was there; I believe all the village shops, the Upton Hotel pub, as well as the Blue Star and Palmer's *Esso* garages had closed down for the afternoon as the owners wanted to attend this once-in-a-lifetime event.

The Earl of Mayo arriving at the fête with Honor Blackman

All the usual stalls you expect to see at a village fête were there: the Bran Tub, the Bottle Stall, a Lucky Dip, a Cake Stall, a Guess the Weight of the Cake stall, a Guess How Many Sweets are in the Jar stall, and Bowling for the Pig were amongst them.

The afternoon was bathed in glorious sunshine, and probably at around 2pm The Earl of Mayo and Honor Blackman arrived and walked through the site, taking a look at everything and talking to the people until they arrived at a small booth where each gave a short speech, and then Ms. Blackman sat in the shade to sign autographs.

The local gamekeeper, Arthur 'Arty' Clothier had laid down his 12-bore shotgun, taken off his jacket, rolled up his sleeves and was quite an expert at bowling for the pig and I believe he probably won it, much to Mrs Clothier's joy and delight, her husband now smiling and proud.

Honor Blackman signing autographs

It was quite a day, very hot, and the air filled with the wonderful fragrance of ale, straw, freshly cut grass (they mowed the area a day or so before) and a hint of dung from the pig, and probably from a few chicken who would be part and parcel of *every* village fête at the time. It was a wonderful and memorable day and pleasing that my very first colour slides turned out to be a success.

Bowling for the pig

There used to be a Liberal Fête, a highlight of the Upton year,
When ladies sipped their sherry, and the men drank home-made
                                                                beer,
There would be a hoop-la and a bran-tub, with lots of silly prizes,
And someone dressed up as a clown, in the most funny of disguises.

The Earl of Mayo opened one such fête, with Honor Blackman from
                                                        'James Bond',
He the public schoolboy type, and she the actress, blonde,
They went through their speeches, and the villagers clapped their
                                                                hands,
Mum looked at me and smiled, and so did my old Gran.

And then the men rolled up their sleeves, it was time to strut their
                                                                stuff,
Bowling balls at wooden skittles, which made them huff and puff,
Called Bowling for the Pig, ya know, the winner'd get that porky
                                                                hog,
Then take him home, tied on a string, just like he would his dog.

The community spirit was marvellous, the whole village would be as
                                                                one,
Twas absolutely nothing like it, everybody had so much fun,
Something rather special, now gone, and it happened once a year,
When the ladies sipped their sherry, and the men drank home-made
                                                                beer.

The village idiot

Not everybody knows this, but there's a contest every year,
To find the village simpleton, a chap who's a little bit…weird,
Not weird the way you think, though, perhaps a little bit unstable,
A chap who's just about as odd, as it says he is on his label.

But contrary to much belief, this is quite some crown to win,
Yet everyone denies it, and thinks that it's a sin,
To be a little bit kind of 'funny', in a peculiar sort of way,
Is quite something, really, despite what they all say.

And it is a secret contest, where no one knows each other,
So your rival could be the man next door, your cousin or your
                                                    brother,
Long as you're dafter than a brush, I'm sure you'll win the prize,
And we'll all know you've won it, cos your head will be twice the
                                                    size.

So when you see an entry form, up Post Office or Down The Hatch,
Pick one up, and have a look, and give your head a scratch,
Fill it in with that there pencil, that's up there on the shelf,
Put it in an envelope, and send it to yourself.

Then you'll know you've won, and you're 'The Idiot' for a year,
And the landlord at 'The Greenridge', will let you buy a round of
                                                    beer,
And most people in Upton village, will think you're quite insane,
When next year you get the form, and do it all over again.

Upton House

Yes, when I watch TV programmes like *Miss Marple, All Creatures Great and Small, The Wartime Kitchen & Garden* or *The Victorian Garden;* I am immediately reminded of Upton in the late 1950s. Okay, it might have been 20 years or so after the period in which Miss Marple and James Herriot's tales of Siegfried Farnon, played by the inimitable Robert Hardy, about their vets practice in the Yorkshire Dales were set, but life hadn't changed that much.

Upton House

Upton House was owned by the Llewellyn family and just after the war my grandmother, Violet Short, worked there as a chambermaid changing the sheets, polishing and dusting, cleaning the silverware and so on. With very little work in Upton as such and with an infrequent 'out-in-the-sticks' bus service and very few villagers owning a car, it was easy to get there by foot or push bike.

During the war, Gran and my Mum, Audrey Short, worked at the munitions factory at Holton Heath. Granddad, Charlie Short, was Station Master at Hamworthy Junction. The family had moved from St Margaret's Road, near *The Tatnam* pub in Poole, to Upton, to be closer to his job. Gran and Granddad also ran a 'Bed & Breakfast' to earn a few extra shillings, and during the war, like many families in Upton, they had two evacuees from London staying with them.

Charles Joseph Short (1888-1953)
Hamworthy Station Master

It was still a time, much as some of those TV programmes tell, of some degree of poverty and having to make do and mend. Charlie Short earned a guinea a week, (£1.05p), and paid 17/6d (seventeen shillings and sixpence, or 87½p) for the mortgage so 3/- (three shillings, or 15p) a week didn't tend to go too far. Things seemed expensive then, relatively speaking, but they were made to last. With no credit cards available and everything paid for upfront, if you didn't have the money to buy the goods, you went without.

Charlie Short, however, like every other man at the time, knew how to help make that small amount of money go as far as possible. With snares set down the railway line towards Hamworthy and even, discretely, into the grounds of Upton House, rabbit would be on the dinner table quite frequently in place of the meat which either they could not afford to buy, or were unable to get due to rationing. Catching a pheasant by hand was and never is the easiest thing to do, unless you were driven to by hunger, of course. It was not unknown for Charlie to catch one on occasion, and, daft as pheasants are wandering around in the middle of roads and suchlike today, they were just as daft then, and to their detriment but to the good-fortune of the family, they helped fill those rumbling tummies.

I don't remember Charlie as he passed away when I was about 18 months old, but I am much like him in my ways, or so I have always been told, both as a child and an adult. He was interred in Hamworthy Cemetery next door to *The Red Lion* pub. From time to time I call in and stand by his grave for a few minutes, drawn perhaps, by that invisible link via our genes, and knowing how both he and I drove my father mad with our casual yet caring way of not worrying about very much at all, as if some inherent knowledge tells us everything will turn out all right anyway.

In that very same churchyard, also tinged with sadness, are the graves of my step-grandfather's two sons. Tom Elliott, a man who worked all of his life on the local railway and was Charlie's lifelong friend, married my Gran after both his wife and Charlie died. Both of Tom's sons were killed during, I believe, the First World War. Tom rarely showed any emotion but having your late-teens to early-twenties family wiped out like that just as they had achieved adulthood must have been absolutely devastating. There, perhaps halfway down towards the left hand side of the cemetery is the Elliott family grave.

Neither my Gran, nor step-Granddad Tom, were buried in Hamworthy churchyard, which I have always found odd. For some strange reason, both chose to be cremated instead of their remains being laid to rest with their families. Who are we to question their wishes but I feel Charlie Short and the Elliott family wife and sons would rest far easier with their kith and kin laying beside them. But as they say up North, "there's nowt as funny as folk!"

The Upton Scouts' bonfire

We were never Boy Scouts, but somehow we got invited,
Perhaps the old Scout Master, was a little bit short-sighted?
It was near the lake, at Upton House, and it was jolly dark,
Creeping around, it was such fun, and something of a lark,
And as we moved closer, the fire was bright and red and hot,
And some kid fell in the lake, he really was a clot,
And every local kid was there, everyone from school,
Then we were told, we must obey, the strictest firework rules.

The Scouts were making cocoa, in great billycans, on the fire,
Then some idiot stunk the place out, by throwing on a tyre,
Rockets whooshing upwards, jumping-jacks around our feet,
Then bread came out for toasting, so we had a bite to eat,
Everything was lit up, with sparks and bangs and colours,
And Melly got knocked over, by his identical twin brother,
The Scouts shared out the cocoa, twas so hot it burnt my tongue,
And it was quite a joy to see, so many people having such fun.

Our faces hot from the fire, it was quite an amazing night,
No one was hurt or injured, or had their trousers set alight,
Then the sky went dark, cos all the fireworks had been fired,
And it was almost ten o' clock, and we were getting tired,
So we started on our way back, towards the safety of our homes,
With more than a few complaints, and half a dozen moans,
But we had such a lovely time, and I'm sure we'll all remember,
The year we joined the local Scouts, for their bonfire in November.

The village grocers

Hicks was the Upton village grocery shop situated where *Custom Kitchens* now stands and adjoining it, now *Palmer Snell Estate Agents,* was a hardware shop where we would be sent, about once a week, to get a gallon of paraffin for the *Valor* heater. If ever we ran out of paraffin, we would have to get dressed for school in a teeth-chatteringly cold home, as hearth fires were never permitted to burn through the night. This was not only for safety but it also to saved on fuel.

Upton Post Office c.1900

Along the alleyway and behind the hardware shop was the village bakery, at one time owned by the Pavey family. One of the delights, not only of this bakery providing gorgeous freshly baked bread, was being sent to the shop to collect it. The loaves, wrapped in tissue paper, would still be hot when carrying them home, which was great in Winter. Mum would take the loaves, one usually being a cottage loaf, and unwrap them, then smile, asking, "They've still got the mice up at the bakery, then?" The mouth-watering fragrance of this freshly cooked bread was so irresistible, it would only be the strongly-willed who could make it home without picking a lump off and eating it on the way. Mum would laugh this off with the joke about the mice.

Hicks may have been there for many years, but I remember that the Wallington family took over the business, probably in the early 1960s, and Mum continued working at the shop. Wing Commander W.F. Wallington was an excellent man and quite some character. Mum was surprised one day when one of 'Wally's' RAF friends dropped in to see him and found the visitor to be Group Captain Douglas Bader. He was an inspirational leader to all fellow pilots after losing his legs in a flying accident, yet continued flying, *and* was also caught by the enemy. Bader had to release himself from the prosthetic legs to enable him to get out of his *Spitfire* aircraft, and after catching him, they were left scratching their heads at this 'man who flew with no legs'? Bader's time in the RAF, and the loss of his legs in the accident, were the subject of the 1956 film dramatisation, *Reach for the Sky*, starring Kenneth Moore.

Wing Commander Wallington, who lived at the premises with his wife, Margot, and their three children, Anna, James and Eric, would fascinate locals with stories of his life, of flying, being shot down on occasion, then captured and sent to a prisoner-of-war camp, escaping and, with colleagues, making his way back home. In a small English village where young lads like myself had read comics like *Victor* with its stories of heroes from the war, Wing Commander Wallington was a hero we could relate to because he was real, and there to see and listen to, and we thought a great deal of him.

Our own father's stories of the war were familiar by now; mine also served in the RAF and saw action in Wellington and Lancaster bombers. He was being sent to places as diverse as Northern Ireland and North Africa as well and fought within the El Alamein conflict, which caused his partial deafness later in life.

In around 1957, as if to reinforce the public belief that World War III could indeed occur, most people in the area heard about a submarine that had been moored alongside Poole Quay and took up the invitation to visit and go inside. Our parents took us one evening, and experiencing the cramped, claustrophobic conditions and the stench of diesel or marine fuel inside this vessel of war was awful. It caused us to wish, hope and for some pray, for a peaceful future.

Mrs Wallington had a black *Ford Consul* in which she would deliver the groceries around the village. With no supermarkets, everyone would order their weekly groceries from the store. Mum was no exception and like every other wife as she ran out of something she would jot it down. On a Thursday, on our way to school, she would drop the little red notebook off at the grocery shop and the following day Mrs Wallington would deliver the goods, usually in a cardboard box, and leave it on the front doorstep. Nothing ever got stolen from this or any other grocery box Mrs Wallington delivered, and it bears wonderful testament to the honesty of those times.

On Saturday, Mum would either go or send my brother or me with the red book, which had been duly priced item by item and totalled up with the money to pay for our groceries, as Dad had been paid the day before. This is how it worked in the village, and even though Moorland Way had *Grays VG* grocery shop, who tended to service that section of the village, and westwards into Seaview Road, *Wallingtons* looked after the Blandford Road, Yarrells and Sandy Lanes, as well as Palmerston Road. Of course, villagers had their allegiances to one store or the other, but both businesses succeeded in making the village 'tick' as part of the hub of the community.

The Crossroads, Upton c.1900

Mum worked with two other shop assistants during her years at *Hicks* and *Wallingtons* store and there's a rather nice story, which again reflects the honesty of the times, attached to the lady named Joan Whitlock.

Mrs Whitlock, as we had to address her as kids out of respect for our elders, lived off Sandy Lane with her husband, Paul, who owned a TV and radio repair shop in Wool. They had a grown-up son, named Cledwyn, an unusual name, but it reflected Mrs Whitlock's Welsh background.

Cledwyn was a great bloke; he had jet-black hair, was handsome and dressed much like TV's *The Fonz* (blue jeans, black boots, shirt and black leather motorcycle jacket). He'd had a motorcycle accident, broken either or both legs, and was recuperating. Whilst he did so, Cledwyn cycled a ladies bicycle from Sandy Lane to where we lived. It was probably Mrs Whitlock's bicycle anyway and as they worked together and got along well, Mum had agreed to let Cledwyn 'park' the bike against the front wall of the bungalow whilst he took the bus into Poole or Bournemouth.

Late one evening (it couldn't be *that* late as there wasn't a bus beyond about 9.30pm) he arrived back and found the bike had disappeared. Annoyed, he walked along Yarrells and Sandy Lane to get home and Mrs Whitlock obviously told Mum the story of the 'stolen' bike when they met up again at the shop.

So, Cledwyn resorted to walking the distance and if we noticed him walk by on his way to the bus stop, we would exchange a wave and a smile. Then, one morning, a couple of weeks later, we noticed the bike had reappeared. It was leaning against the bungalow's front corner-wall *exactly* as it always had. We went out to have a look to make sure we weren't seeing things, and yes, it was the same bike, but it had an envelope hanging from the handlebars by a piece of string. Mum hurriedly opened it and it read something like this: 'I'm sorry about taking the bike. I'm a marine stationed at Rockley and I needed to get home as my wife was having a baby and it meant I'd get there faster. Sorry if it caused any problems.'

Mrs Eades' sweetshop

Where the doctors and the library are, stood the sweetshop of Mrs
Eades,
A veritable cornucopia, of all the children's needs,
With row upon row of sweet jars, filled with bulls-eyes and bubble
gum,
And if you'd spent your pocket money, then you'd have to creep
around your Mum.

Lemon sours and sherbet fountains, we never knew which ones to
buy,
And if we ever weren't too sure, she would give you one to try,
If you liked it, you would nod your head, then she'd weigh them on
the scales,
Whilst she and Mum swapped gossip, about the current village tales.

Those sweets were always in paper bags, nothing was ever pre-
packed,
And she never seemed to run out, always plenty more out the back,
She had a smiling face and glasses, and a head packed tight with
curls,
And Mrs Eades was the favourite place, for all the Upton boys and
girls.

We would go there straight from school, for an ounce of Rainbow
Drops,
Or a great big bag of penny chews, or a couple of sweet lolly-pops,
Then one day, she disappeared, Mum said she'd gone to Leeds,
And we never did find out, what happened to dear old Mrs Eades.

Probably, she had passed away, and Mum didn't want us being
upset,
But now we didn't have a place to go, to buy our sweet cigarettes,
Then the old shop was demolished, just like the blacksmiths next
door,
A little piece of Upton's history, that we couldn't enjoy any more.

The butcher's shop

Yes, Upton had a butchers shop, I don't know if you knew?
Now 'Layers' hairdressers is here, with much the same long queue,
And Mr Cooper owned this shop, he'd sell you any kind of cut,
Well, least ways when he was open, he couldn't when he was shut.

Mr Cooper had a massive chopper, to cut up his joints of meat,
And all the housewives admired it, yet he was far from cheap,
They went in there quite often, for a pound of Cooper's sausage,
Or mince for their cottage pie, if he hadn't run out of cottage.

A pound of finest brisket, or a couple of nice pork chops,
Mr Cooper would serve you well, his meat was never a flop,
It always tasted beautiful, be it pork or beef or lamb,
For the finest cuts in Upton, Mr Cooper was 'the man'!

Then super-dooper-markets came, and Cooper's queue went down,
You'd get much more at Tesco, for your hard-earned half-a-crown,
So he rode off into the sunset, with his cutlery shiny and bright,
And another special part of Upton, had vanished over-night.

Rhode Island Reds

An earlier chapter mentioned dripping, which was the term used for the fat that had emerged from, usually, a joint of beef, whilst it had been cooking. Dripping was delicious in bread or toast, and was one of the key foodstuffs used to keep people warm in the Winter.

Beef was the most common meat just after the war, available for a Sunday lunch or late afternoon dinner. These days, chicken is the most common meat for a meal and beef is regarded as an expensive luxury.

But the thing was, during and after the war, when folks had turned their gardens over to growing fruit and vegetables to eat, they had also been encouraged by the Government to keep chickens for their eggs as these had been rationed. Chickens, therefore, were regarded with an almost god-like status and, as anyone who works in a supermarket will tell you, eggs are one of the biggest sellers and they shift from the shelves at an amazing rate of knots.

More so then than now, eggs were regarded as one of the main, nutritious foodstuffs which no one could do without. But there had been times during the war when they had had to, and they were sorely missed. In the past, before supermarkets started selling vast quantities of cakes and biscuits full of additives and preservatives, a large amount of home baking would take place in the kitchen and eggs were one of the main commodities required. So, although dried egg was available for cooking during the war years, it was beneficial to keep chickens. Once the Government gave the go-ahead for this, people were permitted four, usually Rhode Island Reds, if they had the space in their garden or smallholding. Of course, an appropriate hen house and run would have to be made from scrap timber, but this was a welcome job, as people had grown tired of the dried egg powder they had no other option but to use.

Chickens are also great recyclers, even though people didn't see the term in quite the same way as they do now. Chickens would eat any of the scraps the dog or cat couldn't or wouldn't devour from the food table or kitchen and also anything spare from the garden plot. Cabbage leaves not suitable for cooking would be a treat for them, and these would be hung up still attached to the root and stalk of the plant to give the birds some exercise in pecking at the greens. They would also eat any weeds the gardener happened to pull from the flowerbeds or plot. Along with the cabbage and greens in general, this would put extra vitamins into the eggs, making the 'free range' variety popular, even today, for these reasons.

So during and just after the war, the humble chicken would be an extremely hallowed bird and turkey at Christmas was also unheard of, at least, as far as the common man was concerned.

At some time during the year, we would go with Mum to *Holland Brothers* in Poole Road, whose premises stood on the current 'Clayfields' development site, where she would buy a dozen week old chicks or baby chickens. We would bring them home in a small box and had a chicken house ready and waiting for them. Inside the chicken house would be an incubator, which was a large, round affair made from galvanised metal with a small paraffin heater built into it, and this would be lit to keep these very young chicks warm. Of course, they were so cute we wanted every one of them as a pet, but no, they were money in the pocket for Mum and Dad at Christmas time.

Throughout the year, these 'pullets,' as they were called, would be reared-on until just before Christmas, when Dad would wring their necks and then take them on his bike, probably two or three of an evening, around to his customers, who would be family or friends living in Hamworthy, Poole and Lytchett Matravers. He even visited one out near the *Cock & Bottle* pub in Morden.

Considering chicken are now the most common food commodity on our planet, they were, just over half-a-century ago, such a treasured creature and we made sure, every evening just before sunset, that someone within the family had closed down the chicken house. The fox was just as keen on chicken as ever, so he would be prowling around after a free meal for his family and we had to do everything we could to make sure it wouldn't be one of our chickens. I can remember laying in bed, snuggling down to go to sleep and hearing startled clucking and an almighty commotion coming from the chicken house, and Dad muttering to Mum, then putting on a coat and Wellington boots to go charging off up the garden to frighten off the fox.

Relatively crazy

I know we all have relatives, aunties, uncles, Mum and Dad,
They're usually compos mentis, but not my lot, they're barking mad,
When we were young we had Auntie Nell and crazy Uncle Vic,
Who did strange things with his tongue and teeth, which sounded
like a zip,
And then our Uncle George, who was as tall as he was slim,
Dressed up like the man on the cereal box, by the name of Sunny
Jim,
And Auntie May was crackers, she wore her cardie back to front,
And Uncle Alf was just as bad, a completely stupid lump,
And Auntie Jim smoked too much, her ceilings turned quite mucky,
And a lady with a name like Jim, she can't have been so lucky,
But they were all relations, who came and went throughout our
lives,
All we can do is remember our nieces, nephews, cousins and wives,
And they'd send us a Birthday Card, and we'd return the same,
And when Christmas time came around, we'd do it all over again,
And woe-betide anyone, who happened to forget to send a greeting,
Cos it would be on the agenda, when we had the next big meeting,
Of families, who in those days, were closer than they are now,
But over the years, we've lost touch, but I can't remember how,
So we don't see these people, who were much closer than any
friends,
But sometimes I don't miss those folks, who were completely around
the bend,
So if indeed you see some sense, or can see where we went wrong?
Perhaps you'd help me with this jacket, as the sleeves are much too
long,
And all those crazy relatives, they're a good miss, I can tell,
As I bang my head relentlessly on the walls in this padded cell.

The camera club

There are books about Poole with a few photographs of Upton in them, but the reason people didn't take photographs quite so profusely then was, mainly, that before the automatic focus camera had been invented in the mid 1940s, photograph-taking equipment was cumbersome and unaffordable by the general public. The resulting photographs would be rather expensive to process as well so people used the services of a professional photographer.

Although as kids we would find it embarrassing when parents had saved up to have our photo taken, it was quite something of an extravagance. With the advent of plastics, cameras dropped in price and became affordable but the film to put in them was still expensive, most cameras using a 120 or 127 size film, but unfortunately the definition of the resulting photographs was not brilliant.

By the early 1960s, at Lytchett Minster Secondary Modern School, or 'The Manor', my brother and his school friend, Peter Stevens, would enjoy staying behind after 4pm, with other like-minded souls, for the photography club run by science masters Alan Willis and Douglas Alexander. Duly, my brother Robert would save his pocket money to kit out the coal store in the bungalow (which, incidentally, was never used as we had outdoor coalbunkers, so it was just a junk room, really) as a dark room for processing films and prints.

Gradually, he bought an enlarger to make the photos bigger and to fit the size of the photo paper, and plastic dishes for developer, water, and another chemical to 'fix' the print, or stop it from fading once it appeared as an image on the paper.

In the first instance and prior to that stage, he had bought a developing tank in which to develop the actual negatives. To get the film from the camera and into the tank it had to be ensured that no light entered or the film would immediately be ruined. So, to begin with, he would 'disappear' under the bedclothes to do this, but later, with help from Mum's sewing expertise and three layers of thick black cloth, she made a bag in which to do this. This bag was fashioned rather like a large pair of knickers but with just the leg holes through which to slip the camera and the developing tank inside, and then one's hands. The parts to go around the wrists were fitted with tight elastic to stop light getting in and spoiling the film, and to do the business correctly, one had to know how get film into the developing tank with eyes shut, and thus save diving under the bedclothes to complete the operation. Robert usually carried this out in the dark room anyway, just to make double sure every ray of light was excluded.

The old Dorset Clay Products site

Photographs would be hanging up to dry on a little make-shift clothes line, but later, he bought a machine for doing this which dried them electrically, and also flat, as they would buckle and appear unattractive after hanging them out on the line.

So, with today's colour films being processed in an hour in many retail outlets in town 'whilst you do your shopping' along with 'instant photos' in digital cameras and mobile phones, technology has moved forwards in leaps and bounds.

But even so, how many people living in Upton, Hamworthy or Poole bother to take pictures of their surroundings? In days gone by we had the excuse of the equipment being bulky and the processing expensive, yet nowadays taking a photograph is cheap and easy to do but familiar landmarks are disappearing and no-one hardly notices or bothers taking a photo before they do. One day they might wish they had.

The day we walked to Beacon Hill

Gran started making fancy cakes, just the day before,
Mum had made some sandwiches, and one fell on the floor,
If we'd had a dog, he'd have scoffed it, gobbled back his fill,
So that would be one less to eat, when we reached Beacon Hill.

It was no epic journey, just somewhere different for the day,
Something to wear us out, as we walked and laughed and played,
The sun was hot, and we did sweat, and finally we arrived,
My brother sat on an ant hill, and they chewed his bum alive.

Hopping about like a loony, didn't know if to laugh or cry,
Then he tripped right over, and got a pine needle in his eye,
It wasn't funny, really, the spots on his bum went red,
And then when he stood up, a fir cone hit him on the head.

Eventually we started, eating those sandwiches and cakes,
And looking across the hills, twas quite a sight and no mistake,
Then I pulled my fingers, along a woodland fern,
It cut right through the skin, so a lesson then was learned.

And so this really served me right, for laughing at my brother,
Gran didn't look too happy, and neither so did Mother,
We didn't just do one thing wrong, we did 'em by the dozen,
Good job we didn't bring along, our accident-prone cousin!

The golden sun was setting, we'd all had such a good laugh,
Now it was time for home, to have ourselves a bath,
To wash off the dirt and grime, and soak our tired young feet,
And have a lovely cup of tea, so strong and hot and sweet.

Lemonade had been all right, but how we missed our tea,
And Mum and Gran, of course, were the first ones to agree,

We put our flowers in an egg cup, there on the window sill,
To remind us of the time we had, the day we walked to Beacon Hill.

Beacon Hill

The murder house is here!

"The murder house is here!" some kid shouted, with fear upon his
                                                                    face,
As an old Army Land Rover parked, this white caravan in its place,
And a shudder riveted through our souls, it was beyond belief,
For they had sent the school dentist, to look at our mouldy teeth.

So we would file into this caravan, and they'd peer inside our gob,
And even if they found a cavity, it didn't mean they'd get the job,
Because we had our very own dentist, and his name was Mr Myers,
But even he appeared quite lethal, when wielding his surgical pliers.

But dentistry was quite different then, they'd knock you out with
                                                                    gas,
And you'd wake up quite drowsy, unaware of what had come to
                                                                    pass,
And it wasn't very pleasant, no matter what others might tell,
But calling it 'The Murder House' never did go down very well.

And yes those dentists did look strange, with evil glinting in their
                                                                    eyes,
And we looked at one another solemnly, seeing who'd be first to cry,
Some said they were the enemy, whom we'd beaten in the war,
Come back to take us peacefully, but none of us were ever sure.

So we were thrilled when that caravan, was hitched up and towed
                                                                    away,
It wouldn't return for a year or more, but we'd still fear that day,
But meantime we would chew our sweets, and wouldn't give a
                                                                    damn,
About the Land Rover, The Murder House, or the evil dentist man.

Manure and a pint of peas

If you asked a classroom full of 8-year-old youngsters what happens to the bodily waste when they flush the toilet, I doubt if most of them would have a clue. If we asked those same children when they last did any gardening, the reply would be very much the same although there would, probably, be one or two exceptions. But little would those very same children know that had they been born in 1900 instead of 2000 how they would offer a thoroughly proficient and dare I say it 'hands on' answer to both. As the children of the family they would have been expected to have helped out in dealing with both jobs. They barely had shops back then never mind supermarkets, so much like during the two World Wars and just after, as I have already mentioned, a home and garden would be pretty much self-sufficient and it had to be. Fair enough, if your runner beans grew better than the family down the road, and their carrots were better than yours, you'd agree to grow a little more of each and swap when harvest time arrived.

But the one thing which made those gardens, and the plants and vegetables in them thrive, was manure, and before we enjoyed the luxury of pulling a chain to get rid of it, *our* manure would be dug into the garden soil to help produce better crops. What else could they have done with it? With the toilet out in the back garden consisting of a small wooden shed, a plank with a hole cut in it jammed across its width and a bucket underneath; there were no more options for this liquid and solid manure but to dig it into the garden? Unsavoury as this may well sound to every generation, those youngsters in particular whose job it was would be pulling a face and saying "Yuk!" well before the rest of us.

To make this 'manure' look a little bit more pleasing and to cut down the odour, the spent ashes and cinders cleaned out from the grate in the front room hearth after the last evening's fire would also be deposited into the same bucket. As with every working garden, it is never finished, it is always what we call 'work in progress', because gardens are growing and evolving all the time; so there would be a trench across the garden into which this bucket of waste would be tipped on a daily basis. Probably at the weekend, when the man of the house had a day off (Saturday was usually worked as part of the standard week, which would be of 48 hours) he would get the spade from the shed and dig the 'manure' in to avoid any more odours coming from it and to keep the flies at bay. Whilst doing so, depending on the time of year, he might plant some potatoes or cabbage or whatever, and the manure would help in growing a better crop.

Indeed, wouldn't it be interesting for some of those people from the 1900s to return to see everything 'disappear' when the chain was flushed; they would probably wonder where it went, and ask why we were wasting such a valuable garden commodity?

Speaking of gardens, a great deal of people with large plots are returning to growing their own produce; with some even keeping chicken. Buying seed these days from most of the local nurseries and shops is much as it always has been in the past for most kinds of plant except the runner and the broad bean, and the humble pea. Yes, they are sold in packets of perhaps 50 seeds in each, but years ago they were sold by the pint! That's right, by the pint. I can remember walking to the *Moorland Way Ironmongers*, then owned by Ron Neil, to buy sometimes a pint of each or perhaps a pint of one and half a pint of peas, as you got more for your money because they're small. And the shopkeeper would grab a brown paper bag, and with a one pint glass beer mug or tankard, would bale out the required pint or half pint from a large bag of the appropriate seed. They did much the same at *W.E. Boone* in Poole High Street. My wife, Jane, originally from Cheltenham, was quite astounded when I told her beans and peas, also known as pulses, were bought by the pint or half pint years ago; maybe you are, too?

W.E. Boone in Poole High Street

Although not an Upton shop, *W. E. Boone* in Poole High Street must be given more than a casual mention. Walking through the shop front door is like going into a time-warp, as the shop has barely changed, (except for the staff, of course), since I can remember. It even has the wonderful yet curious fragrance of earth, timber, plants and seeds and all things good; and is worth walking in there for that nostalgic trip back in time, alone.

The chimneys of Factory Road

Three chimneys on the skyline, down the Factory Road,
Three mighty kilns beneath them, fired up by tons of coal,
And they would belch their smoke out, each and every day,
To bake the pipes inside them, made from Upton's clay.

The coal was delivered, by steam trains from the Junction,
Shunting the trucks in and out, took quite a bit of gumption,
But we would watch in awe and wonder, the best bit of our day,
And then they closed the railway down, and took the rails away.

And Dorset Clay survived a while, until something quite drastic,
With the advent of oil and its derivatives, the boffins invented
plastic,
So clay pipes went out of fashion, because they so easily broke,
And then they knocked the chimneys down, so they'd no longer
smoke.

Another Upton era gone, and they built factory units in Factory
Road,
The Dorset Clay Products lorries, had taken out their very last load,
And now it's just a memory, to those locals, who might be you?
Who remember when Upton had industry, and a railway passing
through.

Clay mining in Upton

Of course, the railway traffic and the railway line running parallel to the main Blandford Road was a constant source of interest, especially if your back garden was a matter of 20 feet or so away from it.

Factory Road didn't have the scores of industrial units it has today; it had but one huge factory with three brick-built chimneys dotting the skyline as a local landmark. It was called Dorset Clay Products and every gardener living close to Factory Road would be all too willing to agree that the area is smitten with more than its fair share of clay. This was an ideal site for the open-cut, surface mining of it for the manufacture of the various clay products.

The Dorset Clay Products site in action

The main open-cut 'pit' had been gradually worked away from the main factory. After a number of years it ended up

61

beneath what is now the *Southern Print* complex of factories at the lower, Hamworthy, end of Factory Road. Day in and day out the cranes would dig out the clay, dropping each bucketful into the cast iron trolleys on a never-ending 'pulley' system, and these would be winched up to the main part of the factory, and tipped. The majority of the clay would then be pressure forced into a piece of machinery which manufactured the straight, collared, 3 foot long clay drainage pipe, and a local lady named Doris Broom spent many years at this job.

The clay pit at Dorset Clay Products

These pipes, manufactured en-masse, would then be transported to one of the three kilns for firing, and Mervyn Strand and John Phillips were the two men who loaded and unloaded the kilns. It was a skilled job to get this part right.

Before anything oil-fired had been invented, the kilns were coal-fired and the coal would be delivered by train in trucks into the railway siding, which was situated where the back wall of the *Rediset* building now stands. The goods train delivering the coal trucks would unhitch the complete train of trucks, moving forwards as the guard opened the siding gate. The engine would then back into the siding and remove the empty trucks. There was a points system just ahead of the siding gate, and the guard would also work this for the engine driver. The engine would then be reversed, and the full coal trucks would be hitched to the empty wagons, then unhitched from the remainder of the train. The engine driver then moved the train forwards, and the guard changed the points to allow the full coal trucks to be reversed into the siding. With just the empty trucks still attached, the engine would pull out of the siding, the points changed again and the engine reversed back to hitch up the remainder of the train. The railway gates adjacent to *Layers* hairdressers would then be opened and the train would move on to complete the remainder of its journey.

Upton railway gates c.1900

Dorset Clay Products had a ropey old lorry, and a man would park it alongside the coal trucks, then drive a small crane with a bucket attachment to scoop the coal from the trucks into the back of the lorry. The coal would then be moved by the truck and tipped alongside the kilns, where probably Mervyn and John would shovel it in when they were ready to fire them up. Later, in 1963, when many branches of the railway system in the UK were shut down by Dr Beeching, and due to progress and new technology, the kilns would be oil fired in preference to coal. A new, steel-built chimney was erected to take away the fumes.

Other, more complex styles of pipe and drains were also manufactured at *DCP*, and these, made in quite large moulds, needed a good deal of expertise with the skilled hands of the likes of Bill Beard and Tim Westacott to make them. They had to place the raw clay inside the moulds whilst, by touch and feel, they would gauge the correct thickness required of the clay inside the mould. These bespoke types of clay product would be large U-bend drains and suchlike, but nevertheless, Mervyn and John would also find the space inside the kiln amongst the common 3 foot pipes, to fire them.

Of course, not every pipe would be taken from the kiln prefect, and the men tapped them with a small piece of metal, and by ear, could judge by the note produced if the pipe was good or faulty. If faulty, they would be tossed to one side, and then taken to 'The Grog' for crushing. The Grog was a huge upright stone wheel set in motion by the motor bringing the skips of clay up from the main clay pit.

John Westacott, my cousin Richard and I would spend hours throwing these waste pipes into The Grog, as it was fun to watch them being crushed. Some of the broken edges on the pipes would be devilishly sharp, and inevitably, one or all of us would go home with a hand gashed open and blood pouring out. But they didn't bother sending us to hospital for stitches; we just bandaged or plastered the cuts over and got on with life. Somewhere within the *DCP* factory, the resulting powdered clay from The Grog would be used in another part of the production process.

The Clay Factory's demise

DCP also owned a small fleet of trucks to deliver the pipes around the UK. With the whole country just emerging from the under-bed-potty and bucket in the back-garden toilet system, and with localised networks of underground sewers being installed, the time must have been exactly right for *DCP*. Then, with the advent of oil and the advances in science and technology, plastics were developed as an oil derivative making the days of the clay pipe numbered as the more sturdy and unbreakable plastic pipes superseded them, causing *DCP* to close down.

The factory, kilns and chimneys were demolished and the Factory Road site, as it is today, was built. But we had a great time playing there and getting to know the men and women who worked at *DCP*, and it was a lot more fun than any *Play Station* game could ever provide!

Upton Eagles

Down the end of Ropers Lane, there's a cycle speedway track,
Well, it might not be there now, but it was a few years back,
And we'd line up on the concrete, just like they do down Wimborne
Road,
And in our imagination, was the roaring of the crowd.

And we'd pedal just like madmen, on those stripped-down, rusty
bikes,
And fly around there like lunatics, as fast as ever you liked,
And we grazed our bony elbows, and cut our knobbly knees,
But we were 'Upton Eagles' heroes, and everyone agreed.

We'd spend the Summer holiday there, with glory in our heads,
And by dusk we'd be retiring, happily to our beds,
Clapped out from our exertions, on the 'Eagle's' speedway track,
Then the very next day at sunrise, you'd find us going straight back.

And now all these years later, it's hard remembering those days,
When we were young and foolish, and cycle speedway was the
craze,
We moved on, but that track stayed, forever and a day,
And we had such a lot of fun, with that old cycle speed-away.

To 'The Manor'

Travel sickness blighted my early years terribly, and even the short 3 mile trip to Poole and back resulted in vomiting at either end of the journey. So even on school days when it poured with rain, and Mum happened to have 5d for the return bus fare, going by bicycle would be preferable. Not only that, by the time you had walked to the bus stop and waited there, you'd be just as wet, or wetter, than if you'd cycled.

Lytchett Minster Secondary Modern, 'The Manor'

There were rumours going around about Wimborne Grammar School being similar to the 'Billy Bunter' stories, and that the teachers wore the sinister-looking black mortar-board and cloak, like 'Mr Quelch' in the same books, and that they played rugby as well as football. As I was a fan of neither and with my travel sickness in mind, I deliberately fluffed my 11+ Exams to ensure a place at the more agreeable Lytchett Minster Secondary Modern, or 'The Manor,' as it was known.

The Manor was but a short cycle ride away. After seeing the rabble of kids gathering at the Grammar School bus stop at the top of Palmerston Road, and the dirty old, diesel-exhaust-puffing, brown liveried *Bere Regis* coach they packed themselves into, the cycle ride and in the Summer, the walk to Lytchett school and back, was far more agreeable whatever the weather.

A Bere Regis coach from the 1950s

But even then achievements were hard-won, and those that were, were sometimes unwanted. Despite always being in the 'A' stream rather than the 'B' or 'C', the 'Form Leader' job was not a favourite in the first term there, and how they voted me into it is still a mystery. As I was absolutely hopeless at keeping the class quiet when the teacher left the room, which was the main part of the job, it is no wonder the white braid around the blazer and the badge designating a 'Prefect' never came my way in more senior years.

Always good at throwing things from the dirt fights my brother and I would have in the back garden on an almost daily basis, I came third in Dorset at throwing the cricket ball. I had to go to Ferndown, which seemed as if it was at the other end of the world, on a dreaded *Bere Regis* coach ride to the Pamp Hill School Inter-County sports day where, after hitting the previous lad's marker peg, I achieved this.

Back at The Manor and hopeless at football, a blessing in disguise arrived when Mr Mansell, the geography teacher who also did games with us, was on the pitch shouting for me to pass him the football. It was a heavy old leather ball, so kicking it, as asked, it hit him right between the legs, flooring him. From the white, sickly looking face and between gasps for air, Mr Mansell banned me from playing football ever again, ensuring, by conniving with the other games teachers, that I would 'suffer' cross-country running forever more.

But it wasn't the sufferance Mr Mansell had intended. The hard-nuts from our year did cross-country as they knew it was a breeze in that everyone would run until they were out of sight of the school, then walk for about 50 minutes, turn and walk back towards the school, then jog back to the changing rooms. The 'Hard-Nuts' were fine in my book and we got on well. They were just young men with the rebel attitude, as was I, only not quite so vocal about it as they and we couldn't see the sense or put up with the discipline for 'obeying the rules' of football and being on a pitch running around with a bunch of boys, when some of the years' girls went on cross-country.

Between us, someone always had a packet of cigarettes so talking to the girls and smoking seemed far more appealing than football.

Sometimes, one of the lads brought a catapult and a few marbles to see if we could bag a pheasant or a rabbit (yeah, right!) but needless to say the pheasant and rabbit population were not taking anti-depressants for fear of us! The only downbeat thing with cross-country was that the magpie had become regarded as something of a pest at the time, and one of the farmers whose land we crossed had the habit of shooting, then hanging the birds by the neck on one of his farm gates; and it was quite sickening as a nature-lover to have pass this poignant, avian gallows.

Unlike today, though, part of school life was not only learning, but suffering punishments, and Mr Jenkins at the Junior School was not the only one keen at dishing them out. At The Manor, generally, it would often be the more civilised 'writing a thousand lines' but 'the slipper' which would be a hard-soled gym-shoe, would be a regular penance for those boys not wishing to take part in games or PE but in this instance, we would only receive just the *three* whacks. The 'three whacks' were the motivation behind the 'Hard-Nuts' taking part in cross-country, as whatever we happened to get up to was far more fun than playing football or being slippered across the cheeks of your bottom with that miserable gym-shoe - it bloody well hurt!

Twice in my memory, public canings took place where the whole school were ordered to the main hall at The Manor, and the then Headmaster, Brinley Carrington, thrashed two boys' palms with a wicked looking and very flexible cane for being caught drinking at *The St. Peter's Finger* pub during the lunch break, and on another occasion, for being caught smoking. Again, it was better for the culprits if tears were not seen, so maybe those boys ended up emotionally destroyed men, too?

But from time to time we would have to take part in a 'proper' cross-country race around the course, which was probably 2 or 3 miles long, either as an 'Inter-House' or 'Inter-School' competition, though splashing through streams and getting the 'thrill of the chill' by running through a thawing kale field on a frosty morning was extremely exhilarating.

In the 4th Year, Tony (or 'Cheshire' as he was known, as he always had a 'cat-that-got-the-cream' smile on his face), Parker was the only contestant in our 'House', which was York, for the Inter-Boys Discus. The competition needed two from each house to throw and Mr Cooper, the actual games master who also happened to be our Head of House for York, approached me while I was on lunch break to say: "Burridge! Take off your blazer and have a throw to help Parker out, will you, please?"

The cricket-ball-throwing muscles were still good, so I did as asked, lobbed the discus, and won the contest for York House, much to everyone's surprise, none more than my own, and the victory became the only Certificate I ever gained for sport at school.

The Evening Echo round

I'd never known it rain as much, as when I had my 'Echo' round,
Ten bob a week was all I got, just half an old English pound,
But it was nice in Summer, when my skin turned golden brown,
Making up for Winter evenings, when I'd get back home half-
                                                    drowned.

All the way down Yarrells Lane, then up around Greenacre Close,
Wet and windy, frosty and cold, not sure which one I hated most,
But it was part of growing up, that brown ten bob notes all mine,
Ten wonderful shillings weekly, and in my Bank Account they'd
                                                    shine.

Mr Carpenter owned the Post Office, a grocer keen and bright,
And he'd count out our 'Echo's', to make sure we got 'em right,
Such method to his madness, and his thinking right and sound,
Cos he didn't want us selling spares, on our 'Evening Echo' round.

And then I'd go down Shore Road, and it was dark and black as
                                                    pitch,
In Winter it was darker than that, and I'd end up cycling in a ditch,
But Sandy Lane had street lights, but still the shadows played such
                                                    games,
Running icy fingers down my back, it really was quite strange.

The Thursday edition was thicker, and so much heavier to lug
                                                    around,
And nights like that I wondered, if it was worth that half an English
                                                    pound?
But if I didn't earn that ten-bob-note, then some other bugger might,
And anyway, I'd got used to it, and grown to be rather tight.

So if your kids start bugging you, about doing an 'Evening Echo'
                                                              round,
It's not quite so bad these days, cos they earn around fourteen
                                                              pounds,
It'll ease them into the working world, for which they'll be more
                                                              willing,
And they'll earn a darn sight more each week, than my measly old
                                                       ten shillings.

The awful fishing trip

'Gone Fishin' may well have become a well-known tune the year of my birth and a hit for Louis Armstrong and Bing Crosby and for just one day in my life, my parents could have said, "He's gone fishin'" too; but for the rest of my days it has to be "Went fishin' and didn't enjoy it one little bit!"

At the age of 15 or 16 whilst still at The Manor, our then woodwork teacher, Mr Maurice Buck, or 'Bucky' as he was known to us kids, organised a Saturday school fishing trip to Hengistbury Head, near Christchurch. Well, that's where we ended up!

We went somewhere else first, probably in the school bus, but where it was escapes me. Grandmother, Violet Short, had loaned her *Thermos* flask, a huge thing holding a rather pleasing 2 tins of tomato soup, and Pam Warren, who worked at Wallington's grocery store with Mum, loaned the fishing rod. Quite how I had volunteered or agreed to go is still a mystery, as fishing is not a sport which fits snugly within my psyche. There is a skill to catching fish, granted, but doing so had never offered even the merest flicker of interest, and killing creatures never has sat comfortably with me, either, so it was sheer joy when the sum total caught during the whole, long, never-ending day was…one measly fish.

Close to the shore at one point and probably skimming stones across the waves from sheer boredom, Gran's flask fell from the knapsack, landed on the beach and went 'pop'! No hot drinks, Gran would not be amused, either, damn it!

Terry Best was also there amongst the 6 or 7 other school fellows, and as the afternoon wore on and dusk began falling, we decided to build a bonfire from the driftwood on the beach. Bucky was OK about this, and probably lit the thing and then someone had the idea of cooking some live mussels found along the shore in the glowing embers.

Nearby, a couple of the lads had tried fishing from a jetty, which went out into the sea for about 30 feet. Terry prized open a cooked mussel shell with the blade of his pen knife, slipped the cooked mussel onto his hook, then walked out onto the jetty, and made a cast. Within perhaps 5 minutes, he'd made the only catch of the day with a cooked mussel!

The whole day, for me, had been the antithesis of the expected joy fishing should, and does bring to the many. But spending untold hours being cold, wet, shivering and miserable with no hot drinks and a broken *Thermos* flask to own up to, any thoughts of fishing expeditions in the future had ended, quite dramatically and promptly, right there.

The pool at the disused Clay Works site

P.C. Beard

Upton had a new village Bobby, about forty years ago,
He had the latest motorbike, so only his brain was slow,
And he made our lives a misery, and his name became quite feared,
Our brand new village copper, and his name was P.C. Beard.

My mate dropped a piece of paper, when he stepped off of the bus,
It was just a simple accident, he wasn't one for making fuss,
Then Beardy revved his motorbike, and drove along close by,
And said, "If you don't pick that up, I'll poke you in the eye!"

Then we're walking down Moorland Way, and there's dung by
                                                    someone's gate,
And we don't wanna tread in it, cos it's slippery and you tend to
                                                              skate,
So we walk out in the road, you see, and we're going along, just
                                                           talking,
And Beardy's there on his pushbike, trying to arrest us for jay-
                                                          walking!

He was on the push bike then, you see, cos he wrote off his
                                                      motorbike,
Pursuing the course of Justice? No, he'd been cocky as ever you like,
And rode it through a farmer's gate, and twisted the frame all weird,
Oh, so very embarrassing, for the illustrious P.C. Beard.

Then we grew up, and so did he, and he disappeared without a
                                                           trace,
But I don't think us Upton boys will ever forget his face,
I wish he was here for the young kids now, oh my goodness, he
                                                     would be feared,
Cos if you didn't do what Beardy said, he'd clip you round the ear.

Spencer's Hair Salon

It used to be down Moorland Way, in the parade of retail shops,
The only place in Upton where, a man could go to cut his locks,
His nickname was 'The Major', cos Mr Spencer was ex-Army,
With eyes much like a murderer, you couldn't call him smarmy.

But in these days of hair cuts, being a particular trend or style,
No such thing for The Major, perhaps just a casual smile?
And your hair could be any colour, black or brown or even blonde,
Cos there was just one kind of hair cut, at Spencer's Hair Salon.

And we may have had ideas, about how we wanted to look,
But with only just one ragged page, in Mr Spencer's hairstyle book,
There was no conversation, you just sat down in the chair,
And let The Major do his worst, with your lovely head of hair.

So with scissors and with clippers, your hair dropped to the floor,
And where it was once quite curly, it just wasn't any more,
And he did it with such dexterity, and some kids even cried,
Cos the only style in The Major's book, was the short the back and
sides.

So in these days of being pampered, and spoiled with modern style,
It's such a different world today, so just think back for a while,
At how we'd sit there, trembling, as The Major prepared to strike,
When many a lad was out the door, and down the road on his bike.

So we dreaded our next hair cut, as much as we dreaded school,
But our world back then was full of, the strictest post-war rules,
So we'd grit our teeth and reluctantly, sit in The Major's chair,
Cos in Upton there was no other way, for a male to cut his hair.

Poole Park Nursery

Despite staying on an extra year to obtain 'O' Level and CSE qualifications, a profession of any kind in the working world eluded me. Interviews at Winfrith and other industrial places didn't tempt me towards the world of engineering, then one day Mum said, "You enjoy gardening, why not write to Poole Park and ask if they have any jobs?"

A couple of weeks later, after the customary interview, I started work at the Poole Park's Department nursery in Kingland Road, as a junior gardener at £4 a week. Almost straight away, I bumped into an old school friend whom had left The Manor the year before, Terry Best from Corfe Mullen. Terry and I had been playground pals from playing 'flick cards' together. The fashion had gone out at the time, but in earlier years cigarettes had a card inside each pack, usually in a series of 48 or 50, with titles like 'Wild Flowers', 'Garden Flowers', 'British Birds', 'Aircraft', 'Flags', even 'Air Raid Precautions' all manner of topics with a beautiful picture on one side of the card, and an appropriate description on the back. The cards were still common enough to be collected, and Terry and I, amongst other school friends, did so.

The tea Mum bought for the family to drink, usually loose as tea bags hadn't yet been invented, also had cards in each pack, and *Brooke Bond, Hornimans* and *Ty-phoo* teas mimicked the cigarette card fashion with topics ranging from 'Out Into Space' to 'Transport Through The Ages' or 'On Safari' with Desmond Morris, and more 'Wild Flowers' and 'Wild Birds'. Each card was an absolute cornucopia of fantastic, colourful artwork with those descriptions on the back from which many a person I have met since has declared, "I learned more reading the backs of those fag and tea cards than I ever did at school!"

So Terry and I had a friendship going by swapping cards to make up sets we were collecting from either the cigarette or tea series, and with the 'swaps' we would play this game called 'flick cards'. With the cards we had doubles of and hadn't found anyone to swap them with, we would find an appropriate wall in the playground, and 'flick' the top card from the pack so that it flew through the air, rather like a helicopter rotor blade, and landed on the ground against the wall. Each person would take turns until one of the flicked cards covered all or part of one of those on the ground. When that happened, whoever's card it was scooped them all up as the prize. It was fun, it was something of a social event and a way of making friends with people who were either younger or older rather than sticking to those actually in your form.

Post-war discipline was in place in the Poole Park nursery, much like our school teachers dished out, and the junior gardener had every miserable job they could think of lined up for him. This was a great relief for Terry, as he'd been doing them for a year, and now it was my turn, even though he would help out with some.

They had a coke-fired boiler to heat the greenhouses, so the first job every weekday morning at 7.30 was for Terry and I to clean it out. The boiler was housed in a concrete pit about 8 feet down to one end of the potting shed, so I would climb down a steel ladder which was set into the wall, to face the fire-breathing monster. It would need 'turning over' and the 'clinker' raked out from underneath the fire grille and shovelled into a bucket. Terry would be at the top to haul up the bucket. The red-hot clinker needed hosing down, so great clouds of steam filled the potting shed whilst this took place. Usually, the senior gardeners would attend to their greenhouses whilst we juniors did this. Terry would tip the clinker into a huge, and I do mean HUGE wheelbarrow, and it would be emptied in a designated area in the yard to cool off, and later be disposed of.

That done, the enormous wheelbarrow would then be used to wheel a further supply of coke from a massive heap of it in the yard, around to the brick-lined chute, down which it would be tipped ready to be shovelled into the boiler during the day. The irony of this is, a few years later the boiler was changed to oil-fired, and as the greenhouses were heated for the hundreds of thousands of geranium cuttings we would take, they later found it was cheaper to grow the geranium from seed. We took geranium cuttings during September, (trailer loads of them would be brought in from every roundabout in the Borough of Poole, by Brian Cooper, who now looks after the flower beds around Upton), so the greenhouses needed heat until perhaps early May. But the double-irony was, when they changed to growing the plants from seed, they could start growing them in late February or early March, and thus save the need for a boiler (except for the tropical greenhouse, of course) for a good 6 months.

I was given my own, unheated greenhouse to look after, and if the foreman, Peter Gates, stuck his finger in any of the pots and found them to be either too wet or too dry, he would grab a water can and, if I was busy working he would tip the water over my head, or if I caught wind of his actions and ran, he would chase me around the nursery whilst trying to douse me at the same time.

They had all kinds of tricks for the junior gardener, like

sending you to the mess room with a galvanised metal bucket inside a polythene bag; when, if you were daft enough, you would boil the kettle, fill the bag / bucket with steam, and bring it back to the potting shed for dipping and sterilising the geranium cuttings. Another one would be sending you to the office to ask for 'The long stand' which they said would be needed for the next job. Of course, George Rendell in the office would be wise to this, and would say, "OK, well just wait there, Bruce (Vickery) has gone to fetch it in the van." So you would wait, and if you didn't see the nurserymen in the greenhouses laughing at you, well, you could be there waiting and getting 'A Long Stand' until George told you to return to the Potting Shed because he thought you had been standing there for long enough.

On another occasion, they would try and convince you to cycle the Parks Department bicycle down the High Street to the *W.E. Boone* hardware shop to get "A pound of rubber nails, so that we can hammer them in without disturbing the neighbours!" Yeah, right! Also, mainly in Summer, there would be hose-pipe fights spraying one another with water and there was always something like this going on with all manner of jokes and fun-filled moments, usually with the junior gardeners getting the raw end of the deal.

The Borough of Poole Parks Department also had another nursery behind the old outdoor Poole baths in Park Lake Road, where the Bellis daisies, wallflowers and quite a selection of shrubs were grown to decorate the roundabouts and flower beds throughout the Borough. But the nature of the sandy soil, in what was called 'The Bottom Nursery', dictated the common weed would be a small stinging nettle. One of the 'old boys', Tom Humphries, decided to tickle the stinging top of one between Terry's thighs while he was wearing shorts. Of course, Terry went mad, but you can guess what's coming next when I tell you that Tom had a bald head and being Summer he had no hat on. Yes, Terry grabbed another stinging nettle and rubbed it across Tom's bald patch. Tom then promptly grabbed his hoe and chased Terry around the nursery with it, screaming and shouting abuse. The stinging nettle 'bites' on Tom's head were like fried eggs and as nasty as the actions by both men were, it still makes me laugh like a drain every time I think about it.

The Marine Camp at Rockley Sands had a great deal of social events and dances, and would hire potted plants and troughs to decorate the front-of-the-stage area in their hall or canteen or wherever they held the dance. These would be collected in an Army lorry, and returned in the same way and the Marines always left a rather large barrel of beer 'for the lads' as a Thank You. It would be Best Bitter, so for about the next week, the lads, including Terry and I, would be wobbling around the nursery half-drunk as every nurseryman had a pint glass of the stuff stashed somewhere.

When it rained, as it seemed to do so a great deal back then, most nurserymen, but especially Terry and I as the juniors, would be assigned to one of the greenhouses for 'pot-washing duties', scrubbing out dirty flower pots in a galvanised metal bath. It had to be carried out for the geraniums to be 'potted-on' when they came out of their boxes, but they were as endless as the rain and sometimes it seemed as if we were washing flowerpots for weeks.

Of course, the nursery soil would be mixed in the yard, both for boxing the original cuttings and for potting on. For this, they bought-in a massive tipper-truck load of top-soil, and with the volume of plants we handled, it tipped a full load about once a week for these purposes, during the Autumn.

There was a machine called The Soil Steriliser, housed in an open-sided shed. It was an 8 foot long tube, about as round as the mouth of a dustbin, set on a framework to hold it high at one end and low the other, with a small motor to revolve it, and a white spirit-fired burner to sterilise the soil by burning any and all weed roots and seeds. This was an awfully hot and very dusty job, and it would, as we were the juniors, belong to Terry and myself, one shovelling the soil in, the other shovelling the hot, steaming stuff out at the other end. When completed, the dust would have stuck to the sweat on our skin and our hair would be full of it too. We would then have to add and mix the necessary other constituents for the relevant *John Innes* potting compost. Again, Terry and I worked like horses doing this job, whilst the senior gardeners chided and ribbed us about anything they could think of or find fault with. It was a good initiation into the working world, believe me; and all for the princely sum of that £4 a week, less income tax and your National Insurance stamp!

Upton in Bloom

When I first got my allot-ment, it was as long as it was wide,
With someone else's runner beans, all the way along one side,
But all the rest was weeds, and it was such a lot of room,
But I wanted to grow something, for this year's 'Upton in Bloom'.

So I dug it and I forked in dung, you could smell it down 'Peter's
                                                    Finger',
But as soon as it was buried, it didn't seem to linger,
And once the seeds were planted, they grew wonderfully well,
The wallflowers and geraniums had such a lovely smell.

So I planted 'em all around Upton, and the village looked a treat,
And everyone talked about it, wherever you happened to meet,
So Upton is now blooming, and of that we are so glad,
And my wonderful allot-ment, is the best I've ever had.

So if you have chance to get one, put up your hand and shout out
                                                    "Yes!"
The Mrs might not like it, though, cos you bring home such a mess,
But you ain't gotta wear yer wellies, inside her posh front room,
And at least you would have done your bit, for this year's 'Upton in
                                                    Bloom'.

Wages and beer

From my weekly wages, there would be enough to pay Mum something for my keep and buy an LP, usually at *Setchfields* in Poole High Street, but occasionally at *Bourne Radio* or *Poole Music Stores*. These latter two shops were at the Dolphin Centre end of town, with *Poole Music* adjacent to The Regent Cinema, which stood roughly where *Boots the Chemist* is now.

Going to the pub to play darts as soon as we were old enough was another place to shift some of those wages from our pocket and into the landlord's till. Yes, we were young men with the world at our feet and we managed to get a bit 'tiddly' or even seven-parts drunk more often than enough, but we didn't wreck someone's garden or car or whatever on the way home. *We crept,* as quietly as possible so that we didn't get caught, otherwise the old man would give us a right telling off for "showing the family up to be drunks and scallywags!"

With everywhere selling alcohol these days it has become such a problem; it was far more under control the late 1960s. If you wanted a pint, you went to *The Upton Hotel* as it was known then, and ordered yourself one. If anyone wanted to drink at home or perhaps if Mum and Gran needed half a pint of *Mackeson* to include in the Christmas cake or pudding as an integral part of the recipe, it would be bought in the *Off Sales* part of the pub. This was a separate doorway roughly at the centre of the building, and either the barman, barmaid, or the publican would serve the customer. Of course, it was easy to see if anyone was under-age or, for whatever reason, shouldn't be sold alcohol. So there was a very strict control over it and it wasn't the problem it is now.

Likewise, we did our bit for *recycling*, not that we had heard of the word and the encouragement to return empty beer bottles was the one universal thing everyone wants and needs: *money!* When a customer bought a pint of Bitter, or Pale Ale or whatever from the Off Sales, it cost a penny or two more than it would have over the bar, and this extra amount was known as the 'deposit on the bottle'. In other words, the customer paid more to drink the beer at home, but had the 'deposit' handed back as cash when returning the empty bottles.

The Greenridge (formerly The Upton Hotel)

This was an excellent way to recycle the glass bottles, and there would *never* be an empty one left cast in a hedgerow or at the side of the road, because *they were worth money;* and people were far too hard up to let that penny or two escape!

As kids, after Christmas, we would generally be sent, rattling as we went, with a couple of shopping bags full of empty bottles, to *The Upton Hotel* to 'cash them in', and if we ended up with a shilling (5 pence now), which then took 12 pennies instead of 5, then we regarded ourselves as being quite rich and well-off. Usually, as a 'perk', we would get the job of taking our own and Gran's bottles, too, so it was a joyous time and a memorable part of our quite hard-up but far simpler and more enjoyable world.

It would be unfair, perhaps, to say "those were the days" again; every generation has and will have its own "those were the days" of their youth. They are our formative years and, perhaps like Poole Park nursery, although I wouldn't have missed the experience, it was a completely different world. War brings people together, much like adverse weather, and in consequence, it gives everyone a common ground for conversation and if Upton suffered the dogfights or a stray bomb then everyone knew and talked about it. No, we don't want another war to get this camaraderie back into our lives, but it would be nice, in general, for people to be less hostile toward one another. Upton has always been a place for people to smile and say "Hello" when walking around the village, even if you have never seen them before. So let's keep that aspect; the world outside and on the TV screen as our News is a nasty enough place as it is without allowing it to seep into this wonderful village in which we live.

The village darts team

Back in Nineteen-Sixty-Eight, 'The Greenridge' had a different name,
It was 'The Upton Hotel' then, and inside we played a game,
Of darts, you know the sort I mean, and the team were mighty
matey,
Especially if someone happened to score, that magical one-hundred-
and-eighty!

The landlord then, was Paddy Orr, a red-faced chap twas true,
And he would take no nonsense, from anyone, including you,
But he enjoyed our darts matches, even though he didn't play,
And he enjoyed them so much more, if they were home and not
away.

We'd play the team at Sandford, down Wareham or Lulworth Cove,
Warm your fingers afore you play, by that there great big stove,
We did our best to win, of course, and enjoy the local beer,
And if one of our boys won his game, there'd be such a mighty
cheer.

And so we travelled all around, playing darts at all these pubs,
With a buffet of nice sandwiches, or perhaps a ploughman's lunch,
Then throw our darts and try to win, or even do quite well,
For our local village team, at the old 'Upton Hotel'.

We were no 'Crafty Cockney,' Jocky Wilson or 'Phil the Power,'
It was just a lot of fun, a way to spend a couple of hours,
Part of life for us young lads, some forty years ago,
And I often think and wonder, where they all might be now?

The Upton carnivals of yore

They used to drive around the village, on backs of lorries dressed as
floats,
Some looked like a florist's shop, whilst others resembled boats,
Such wonderful community spirit, unheard of since the War,
When villagers worked together, for the Upton carnivals of yore.

And the kids and adults had such fun, in fancy dress and make-up,
too,
And if you laughed a bit too much, next year they'd make sure it
was you,
Yes families; men, women and kids, be they rich or be they poor,
Made those colourful May-Day floats, for those Upton carnivals of
yore.

Some dressed as sailors from the quay, others like St. Trinian's girls,
And little 'uns from The Teddy Bear Club, sat in sea shells, dressed
up as pearls,
The Gardening Club, like 'Bill and Ben', and even 'Little Weed' for
sure,
In the sunshine, with a clear blue sky, in the Upton carnivals of yore.

Then one year they just disappeared, and no one seemed to know
why?
May-Day came, and May-Day went, beneath that sunshine and blue
sky,
The laughter and the fun now gone, everyone looks extremely bored,
Perhaps they are remembering, those Upton carnivals of yore?

Alan Burridge, the author
The man who has made Upton famous with his name and address
on millions of Motorhead album sleeves worldwide!

Upton Crossroads for Visitors was first published in the Autumn 2007 edition of *The Lytchett Bay Post* community magazine.

The Village Idiot was first published in the Spring 2008 edition of *The Lytchett Bay Post* community magazine.